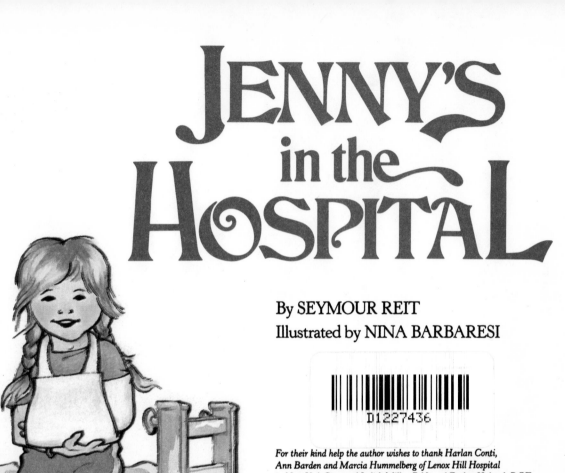

JENNY'S in the HOSPITAL

By SEYMOUR REIT

Illustrated by NINA BARBARESI

For their kind help the author wishes to thank Harlan Conti,
Ann Barden and Marcia Hummelberg of Lenox Hill Hospital
in New York City, and Judith Miller, R.N. and Evelyn Halsted, R.P.T.
The illustrator wishes to thank the members of the staff
of Greenwich Hospital in Connecticut.

A GOLDEN BOOK, NEW YORK

Western Publishing Company, Inc.
Racine, Wisconsin 53404

One Saturday afternoon,
Jenny was at the playground
climbing on the jungle gym.
   "Look at me, Mommy!"
she called.

Suddenly Jenny lost her balance. She fell down to the ground, bumping the back of her head and landing hard on her left arm. Jenny's arm hurt. So did her head. Her mother thought she ought to see a doctor right away.

Jenny and her mother took a taxi to the emergency room at a nearby hospital.

The doctor who examined Jenny's arm decided to take x-rays. He needed to know if Jenny had a broken bone.

Jenny was nervous. But she didn't feel a thing when the machine took the x-ray picture.

The doctor studied the picture of the bone in Jenny's arm. "You have a hairline fracture, Jenny," he said. "It's just a tiny break, but we'll have to put your arm in a cast for a while."

"Will the cast hurt?" Jenny asked.

"Not a bit," the doctor replied.

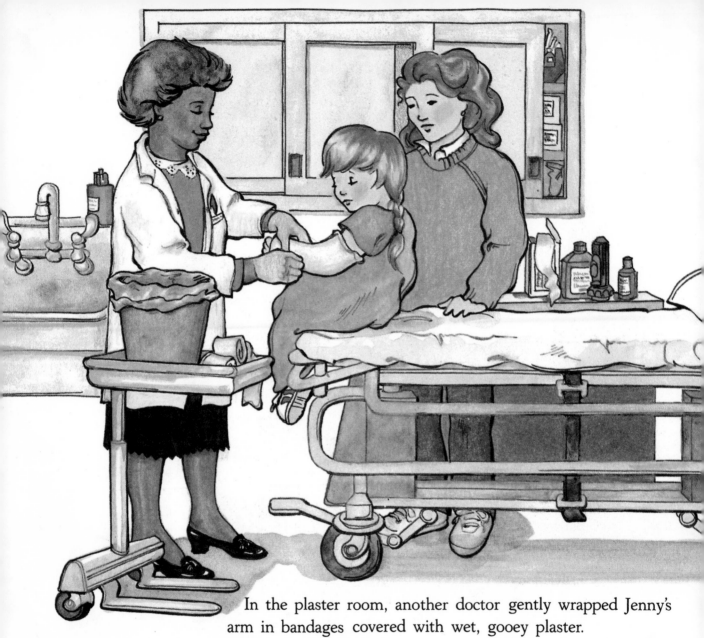

In the plaster room, another doctor gently wrapped Jenny's arm in bandages covered with wet, gooey plaster.

"When the plaster dries," said the doctor, "the cast will be stiff and hard. It will hold your arm still so the bone will be able to mend itself."

Jenny's arm didn't hurt much any more. But her head still ached and she felt dizzy. The doctors decided she should stay in the hospital overnight.

A clerk in the admitting office made a name-bracelet for Jenny to wear on her wrist.

Then Jenny's mother talked to her father on the phone. He said he was coming over right away.

Next Jenny and her mother went up to Pediatrics—the children's area of the hospital. A nurse named Linda Gomez took Jenny to her room and gave her a hospital gown with snaps in the back.

Jenny said hello to the other girls in her room. Ellen was in the hospital for tests. Gloria was going to have an operation in the morning.

There was a menu near Jenny's bed. Her mother helped her choose something she liked for dinner.

After Nurse Gomez helped Jenny into her gown, she took
her pulse, blood pressure, and temperature. She also took blood
from Jenny's finger. "This is for laboratory tests," she explained.

Finally she showed Jenny a button near her pillow. "If you
need me for anything, press this buzzer."

Jenny's father arrived with her things, just as a hospital aide put her dinner tray on the rolling table beside her bed.

"Don't worry, Pumpkin," said Daddy when he saw the look on Jenny's face. "You'll feel like eating by tomorrow."

When it was time for Jenny's parents to go home, they hugged her and said they would be back tomorrow.

Gloria's mother was spending the night. She wanted to stay with Gloria until her operation the next morning.

The night nurse tucked the girls into bed and told them to press their buzzers if they needed her. She would be nearby at the nurses' station, and would check on them all through the night.

By morning Jenny felt much better. Nurse Gomez told her that Gloria had already gone to surgery for her operation. "She'll be back in a few hours."

After Jenny ate her breakfast, Nurse Gomez said she had to see the doctor for a few tests. "Just to make sure your head is really okay," she explained.

A hospital aide named Clifford brought
a wheelchair to take Jenny for her tests.
"All patients have to use wheelchairs,"
he said. "That's a hospital rule."

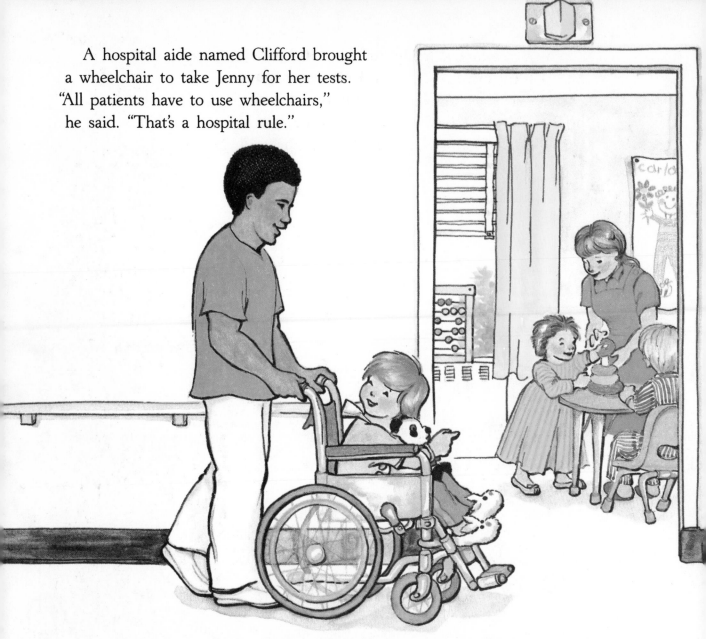

On the way to the doctor's office, they passed the children's playroom.
It was filled with toys and books and games. Jenny wanted to stop there,
but Clifford said they had to go see the doctor first.

The doctor asked Jenny how her head felt. Jenny said it still hurt a little, but she didn't feel dizzy any more.

He told her to move her head up and down, and to wiggle her fingers and toes. He looked into her eyes and ears with a special light. "You're doing fine, Jenny," he said. "You can go home this afternoon."

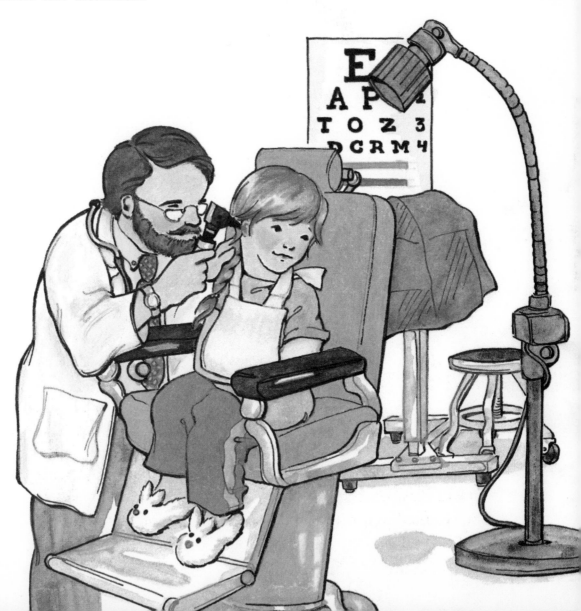

air conditioner

recovery room

operating room

Jenny's room

playroom

examination room

ele

emergency room

gift shop

ambulance

Clifford came to take Jenny back to her room.
But Jenny wanted to go on a tour of the hospital.

laundry

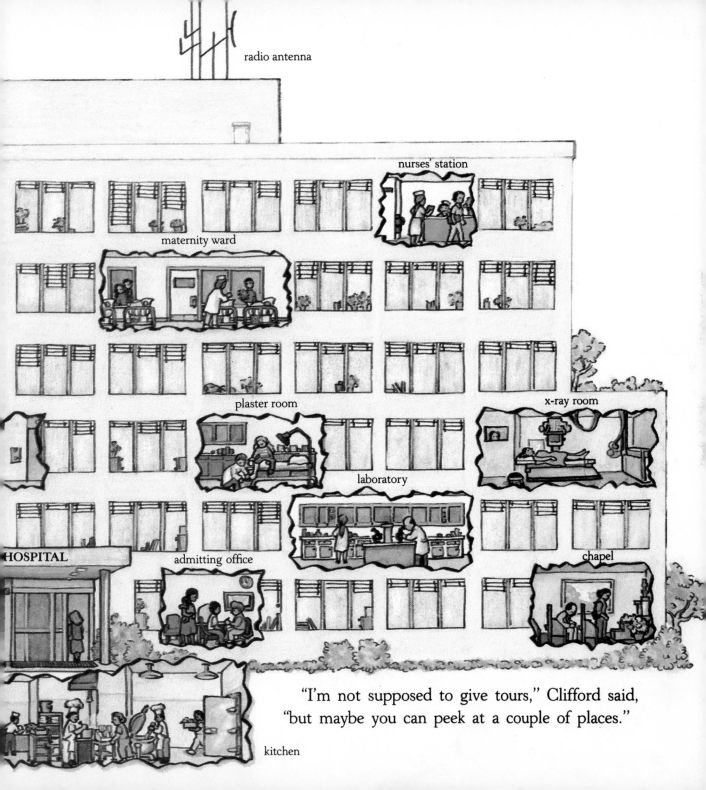

radio antenna

nurses' station

maternity ward

plaster room

x-ray room

laboratory

HOSPITAL

admitting office

chapel

"I'm not supposed to give tours," Clifford said,
"but maybe you can peek at a couple of places."

kitchen

First Clifford took Jenny down to the laundry room in the basement. *Plop! Thump!* Bags of dirty linen came out of chutes from the floors above and dropped into big bins. Workers rolled the bins over to the huge washing machines. Other people were ironing and folding stacks of clean laundry.

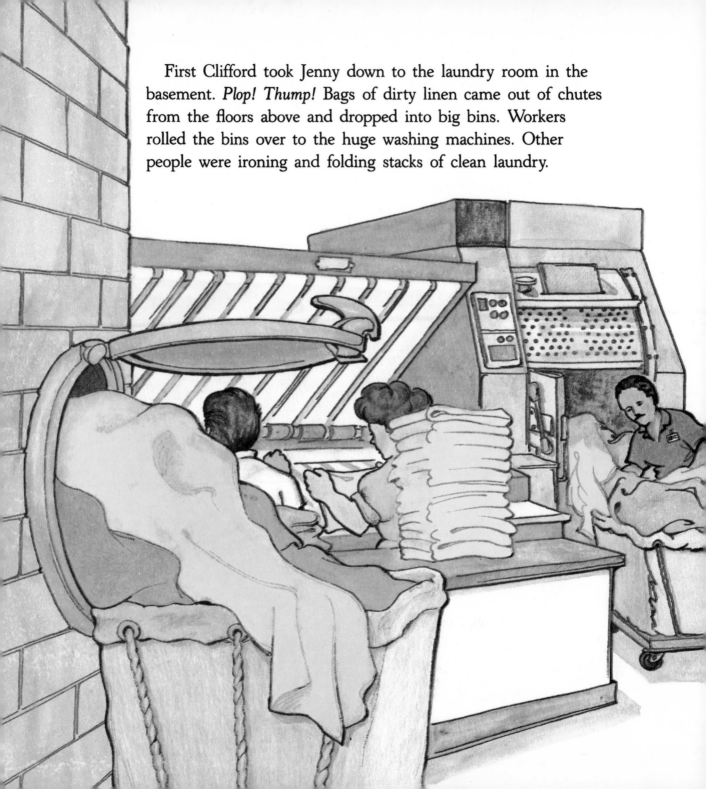

Next Clifford and Jenny peeked into the hospital's busy kitchen. The pots on the stoves were larger than any Jenny had ever seen. And people were walking in and out of the huge refrigerator.

Last of all, Clifford took Jenny
to see the newborn babies in the
maternity ward. Jenny stared through
the windows of one of the nurseries.
Each tiny baby was wearing a little
name-bracelet, just like hers.

"I wonder if I was born here,"
said Jenny.

Then a nurse came by and said
it was time for Jenny to go back
to Pediatrics.

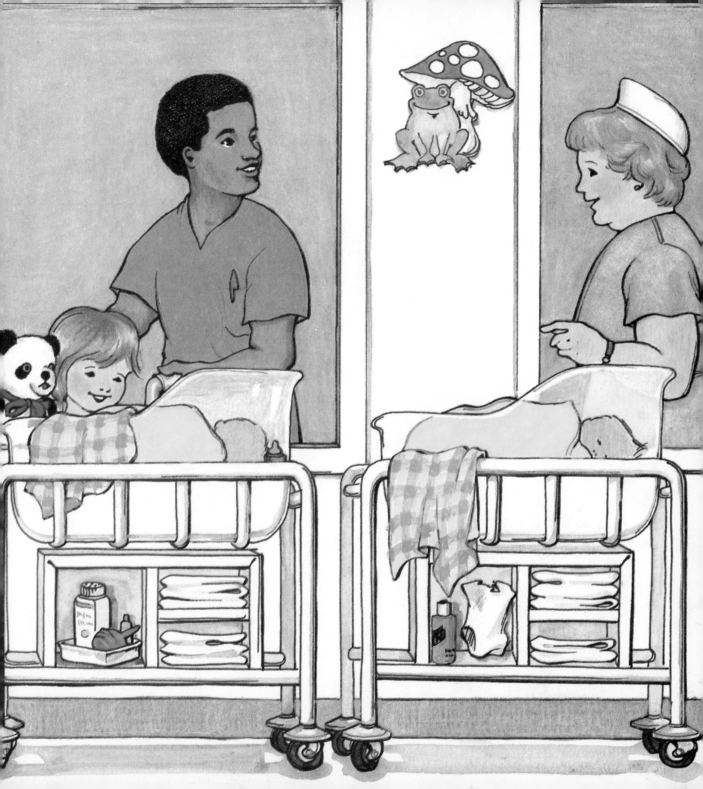

Jenny's parents were waiting at the nurses' station.

"I saw the doctor," said Jenny. "He says I can go home this afternoon." Then she whispered, "Clifford took me on a tour—even though he wasn't supposed to."

Nurse Gomez smiled and shook her head.

PEDIATRICS

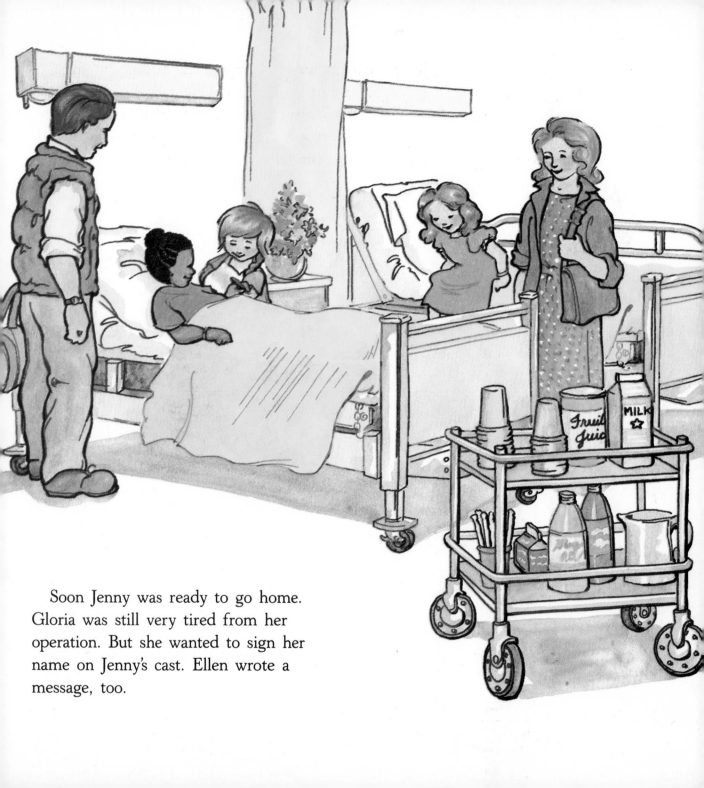

Soon Jenny was ready to go home.
Gloria was still very tired from her
operation. But she wanted to sign her
name on Jenny's cast. Ellen wrote a
message, too.

On her way out, Jenny stopped to show Nurse Gomez what everyone had written. Jenny's favorite message said, "From your friend Clifford, the best tour guide in the hospital."